T0003136

NEW VANGUARD 329

TANKS ON IWO JIMA 1945

ROMAIN CANSIÈRE ILLUSTRATED BY FELIPE RODRÍGUEZ

OSPREY PUBLISHING

Bloomsbury Publishing Plc

Kemp House, Chawley Park, Cumnor Hill, Oxford OX2 9PH, UK

29 Earlsfort Terrace, Dublin 2, Ireland

1385 Broadway, 5th Floor, New York, NY 10018, USA

E-mail: info@ospreypublishing.com

www.ospreypublishing.com

OSPREY is a trademark of Osprey Publishing Ltd

First published in Great Britain in 2024

© Osprey Publishing Ltd, 2024

All rights reserved. No part of this publication may be reproduced or transmitted in any form or by any means, electronic or mechanical, including photocopying, recording, or any information storage or retrieval system, without prior permission in writing from the publishers.

A catalog record for this book is available from the British Library.

ISBN: PB 9781472860392; eBook 9781472860408;
ePDF 9781472860378; XML 9781472860385

24 25 26 27 28 29 10 9 8 7 6 5 4 3 2 1

Index by Fionbar Lyons
Typeset by PDQ Digital Media Solutions, Bungay, UK
Printed and bound in India by Replika Press Private Ltd

Osprey Publishing supports the Woodland Trust, the UK's leading woodland conservation charity.

To find out more about our authors and books visit **www.ospreypublishing.com**. Here you will find extracts, author interviews, details of forthcoming events, and the option to sign up for our newsletter.

Acknowledgments

I would like to thank all the individuals and institutions that contributed to this book, starting with veterans Myron Czubko and Martin Murphy. Chuck Bernard and Sean Winn (Patriot Features) were instrumental in connecting the author with the veterans above. Kirby Nave shared the memoirs and photo album of his father, Bert. Joe Moran shared his father's papers. Akira Takizawa helped in locating Japanese sources and kindly shared his knowledge on World War II Japanese armor. Thanks to Eury J. Cantillo (curator, U.S. Army Ordnance TSF) and Jonathan Bernstein (curator, National Museum of the Marine Corps) for respectively sharing information on the Type 97 preserved at Fort Lee and the Sherman belonging to the Marine Corps museum.

The staffs of the Marine Corps History Division, US National Archives, National Museum of the Pacific War, and National Diet Library (Japan) assisted me in locating a large amount of archival documents, visual and textual. Many thanks to Caroline Cansière who provided key on-site assistance.

Last but not least, I would like to acknowledge my friend and mentor, the late Oscar E. "Ed" Gilbert Jr who transmitted his passion for Marine Corps armored history. He also shared a quantity of material collected over the years, part of which is used in the subsequent pages.

Dedication

To Augustin

CONTENTS

TANKS ON IWO JIMA 1945

INTRODUCTION

The legendary battle of Iwo Jima was fought by some 92,000 American and Japanese combatants. Doctrinally, each side fielded tanks in support of its infantry. With a ratio of more than four US tanks for a single Japanese tank, the battle of Iwo Jima highlights the huge disparity between the American and Japanese armor that existed during the latter part of World War II.

In addition to tanks, the American fighting arsenal benefited from amphibious tanks and half-track tank destroyers. Though they only played a limited role, they added weight to the already overwhelming US firepower.

The following pages intend to shed light on the role of the Japanese and American armored vehicles and their influence on the course of the brutal battle for Iwo Jima in 1945.

TANKS, OTHER ARMOR AND ORGANIZATION

The Japanese

Japanese armor on Iwo Jima consisted of the 26th Tank Regiment commanded by Lieutenant Colonel Takeishi Nishi. The unit was formed in Manchuria in April 1944 from the Reconnaissance Unit of the 1st Armored Division and was intended to be shipped out to the Marianas to strengthen the Japanese forces already in place.

At the time it left Manchuria, it was actually a battalion-strength regiment with some 800 men and 41 tanks.

In June 1944, the regiment was ordered to reinforce Saipan, but before it left the Asian continent, the island was reported captured by American forces. By early July, the tank regiment was reoriented toward Iwo Jima. After a brief stop at Yokohama harbor, Japan, the convoy transporting the tanks shipped out to Iwo Jima on July 10. The 26th Tank Regiment was loaded onto the *Nisshu Maru* and the *Tonegawa Maru*.

Marine Shermans on Iwo Jima were covered with a multitude of additional protections to increase chances of survival of their crews. Here is an A Company, 5th Tank Battalion Sherman with wooden armor on the sponsons and spikes on the hatches. (NARA via Ed Gilbert)

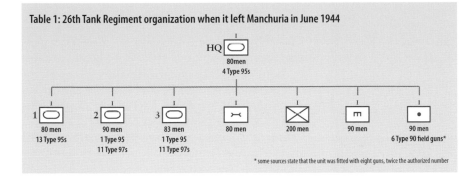

Table 1: 26th Tank Regiment organization when it left Manchuria in June 1944

```
                              HQ  ⬭
                             80 men
                            4 Type 95s
    ┌──────────┬──────────┬──────────┬──────────┬──────────┬──────────┐
  1 ⬭        2 ⬭        3 ⬭        ⊢⊣         ⊠          ▥          ·
 80 men     90 men     83 men      80 men    200 men    90 men     90 men
13 Type 95s 1 Type 95  1 Type 95                                 6 Type 90 field guns*
           11 Type 97s 11 Type 97s
```

* some sources state that the unit was fitted with eight guns, twice the authorized number

The latter vessel reached Iwo Jima on the 14th and successfully disembarked the 1st Company, the artillery, the infantry, and parts of the maintenance and HQ companies. The *Nisshu Maru* was forced back to harbor for repairs and sailed from Yokohama for the second time on July 14.

On July 18, as the *Nisshu Maru* was approaching Chichi Jima (an island north of Iwo Jima) the ship was torpedoed and sunk by the USS *Cobia*, an American submarine. Although most of the troops survived the sinking,[1] the tanks of HQ, 2nd, and 3rd Companies were all lost.

On July 19, the *Nisshu Maru*'s survivors reached Chichi Jima. Lieutenant Colonel Nishi and a detachment of 47 men left Chichi Jima for Yokosuka, Japan, in late August to get replacement tanks for the regiment. The remainder of the unit was transferred to Iwo Jima in September. Finally, some 22 replacement tanks were delivered piecemeal to Iwo Jima between September and December.

In the end, a total of 35 tanks were shipped to Iwo Jima. They consisted of Type 95 Ha-Gos light tanks and Type 97 Chi-Has and Shinhoto Chi-Has medium tanks.[2]

Nishi organized them into three line companies of about ten tanks each, light and mediums, plus a HQ Company with the remainder being light tanks. The 26th Regiment's command post (CP) was located east of the second airfield, in the vicinity of the village of Motoyama. When the Americans landed on February 19, the three tank companies were located as follow: the 1st Company was east of Motoyama, the 2nd Company east of Hill 362A, and the 3rd Company entrenched south of the third airfield. The artillery and engineer companies were split between the three tank companies. (See map on p. 13.)

Initial orders for the 26th Tank Regiment were to maintain their positions until American forces reached their lines.

The Type 97 *Chi-Ha* was designed in 1937 and was classified as a medium tank despite its weight (14 tons). This is one of the 22 replacement vehicles sent to Iwo Jima by late 1944. The tank was knocked out by American bombardment while still aboard its transport ship (top photo). Japanese soldiers reported that the tank burned for two days after being hit on Christmas Eve, 1944. (NARA)

---

1   Only two men from the 26th Tank Regiment died in the sinking.
2   Three tanks were eventually knocked out by the US preliminary bombardments (aerial and naval), leaving some 32 functional Japanese tanks when US troops landed. The exact number of tanks of each model is unknown.

The light tank Type 95 Ha-Go was more than obsolete by 1945 with its mid-1930s design. It was crewed by three men and was equipped with a 37mm main gun. This Type 95 was hidden in a crevice near Hill 382, east of the second airfield. (MCHD)

The Americans
Amphibious tanks

The 2nd Armored Amphibian Battalion was designated to support the two Marine assault divisions on D-Day on Iwo Jima.

The unit, a veteran of the Marianas campaign, was equipped with 70 LVT(A)-4 amphibious tanks, which were basically an LVT(A)-2 mounting a 75mm howitzer in a rotating central turret. It was capable of movement both on land and in the water, propelled by its W-shaped tracks. Floatability was made possible by sacrificing the vehicle's protection, having just ¼in.-thick armor.

Amphibious tanks made their first appearance in the Marshall Islands campaign to provide immediate support to the first waves of attacking infantry. They usually preceded the first wave of ground troops, reducing enemy opposition on and around the assault beaches. They provided close infantry support until tanks with heavier armor and more powerful guns were debarked.

On Iwo Jima, the battalion was divided into two equal components: C and D Companies (with 17 LVT(A)s each) supported the 5th Marine Division, and A and B Companies (with 17 LVT(A)s each) supported the 4th Marine Division. Each group also had one LVT(A)-4 from the H&S (Headquarters and Service) Company.

The objective was for LVT(A)s to set up firing positions past the first terrace after landing and fire at targets of opportunity until ground troops masked their fire.

Tank Destroyers

Within its Weapons Company, each Marine (Infantry) Regiment possessed four or five M3 Gun Motor Carriages (GMCs). These were half-track vehicles equipped with a 75mm gun. Although they were designed as tank

A

1. TYPE 95 HA-GO (EARLY), 26TH TANK REGIMENT

This vehicle most likely belonged to the original 1st Company that safely reached Iwo Jima in the summer of 1944. The tank shows the pre-1942 jungle camouflage made of grass green and brown colors, with a yellow disruptive stripe. The original unit symbol, called "the Blue Spear," was designed in mid-1943 by the Reconnaissance Unit of the 1st Armored Division and later inherited by the 26th Tank Regiment. It was painted on tank turret sides. Highly visible, the unit symbol was usually painted over to avoid detection on Iwo Jima. This tank was captured in running condition by the US 3rd Tank Battalion.

2. LVT(A)-4, 3RD PLATOON, D COMPANY, 2ND ARMORED AMPHIBIAN BATTALION

US amphibious tanks were heavily camouflaged with navy gray, red-earth, and olive drab (sometimes black) splotches. Tactical markings consisted of a white letter-number code. The letter indicated the company and was followed by two digits: the first indicated the platoon and the second the vehicle's position within the platoon. A name was also painted in white on the forward part of the side pontoons. One or two colored stripes were painted vertically on the sides, front, and rear of the tank, which indicated the beach (Green, Yellow, or Red) and beach number: a single green stripe indicated the vehicle was scheduled to land on Green Beach 1.

The Japanese built up several dummy tanks out of wood, locally found vegetation and even stones. This was intended not only to confuse the Americans as to the number of tanks on the island, but on their location as well. The trick seems to have worked well since by January 1945, American intelligence reported some 40 enemy tanks positioned all around the island. (NARA)

BELOW LEFT
LVT(A)-4s were equipped with a 75mm howitzer main cannon. They were designed right after Tarawa to provide direct fire support to the first waves of Marines on enemy held beaches. Note the armored amphibian sunk in the soft volcanic ash in the background. (MCHD)

BELOW RIGHT
Some 37 M3 GMCs belonging to the three Marine Divisions landed on Iwo Jima. These vehicles were originally designed as tank destroyers, but they seldomly filled this role by lack of appropriate targets in the Pacific. The UNIS marking on the bumper of this 75mm half-track indicates it belongs to Weapons Co. ("02"), 28th Marines ("8"), 5th Marine Division (square). (NARA via Ed Gilbert)

destroyers, they were rarely used as such, and were often deployed in secondary defensive roles in case of enemy counterattacks.

These obsolete vehicles were still in use within the Marine Corps by early 1945, illustrating how disparate the equipment was. The M7 – its replacement – did not arrive in time to take part in the battle of Iwo Jima.

Tanks

The three Marine divisions selected to assault Iwo Jima (the 3rd, 4th, and 5th Divisions) brought in their respective divisional tank battalions. The 4th and 5th Tank Battalions were part of the assault troops, while the 3rd Tank Battalion (like its mother division) was held in reserve.

The US Marine Corps tank battalions on Iwo Jima followed the April 1944 F-Series table of organization, with a theoretical 620 men and

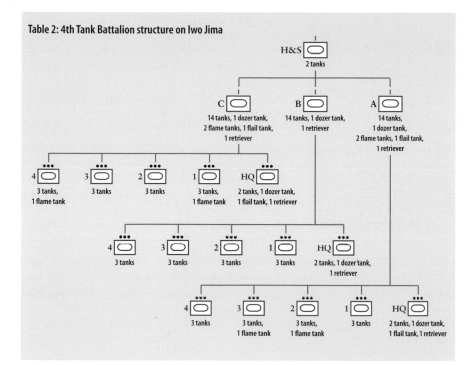

Table 2: 4th Tank Battalion structure on Iwo Jima

H&S — 2 tanks

C — 14 tanks, 1 dozer tank, 2 flame tanks, 1 flail tank, 1 retriever

B — 14 tanks, 1 dozer tank, 1 retriever

A — 14 tanks, 1 dozer tank, 2 flame tanks, 1 flail tank, 1 retriever

4 — 3 tanks, 1 flame tank
3 — 3 tanks
2 — 3 tanks
1 — 3 tanks, 1 flame tank
HQ — 2 tanks, 1 dozer tank, 1 flail tank, 1 retriever

4 — 3 tanks
3 — 3 tanks
2 — 3 tanks
1 — 3 tanks
HQ — 2 tanks, 1 dozer tank, 1 retriever

4 — 3 tanks
3 — 3 tanks, 1 flame tank
2 — 3 tanks, 1 flame tank
1 — 3 tanks
HQ — 2 tanks, 1 dozer tank, 1 flail tank, 1 retriever

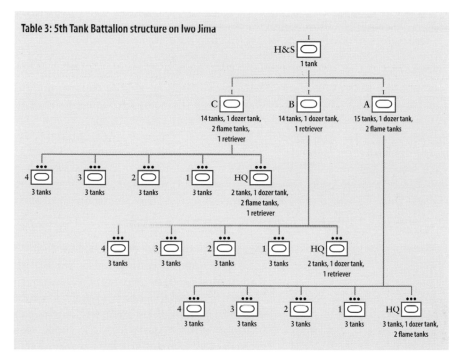

Table 3: 5th Tank Battalion structure on Iwo Jima

H&S — 1 tank

C — 14 tanks, 1 dozer tank, 2 flame tanks, 1 retriever

B — 14 tanks, 1 dozer tank, 1 retriever

A — 15 tanks, 1 dozer tank, 2 flame tanks

4 — 3 tanks
3 — 3 tanks
2 — 3 tanks
1 — 3 tanks
HQ — 2 tanks, 1 dozer tank, 2 flame tanks, 1 retriever

4 — 3 tanks
3 — 3 tanks
2 — 3 tanks
1 — 3 tanks
HQ — 2 tanks, 1 dozer tank, 1 retriever

4 — 3 tanks
3 — 3 tanks
2 — 3 tanks
1 — 3 tanks
HQ — 3 tanks, 1 dozer tank, 2 flame tanks

46 medium tanks plus three retrievers (recovery vehicles). A tank company would theoretically comprise five platoons of three tanks each.

In actuality, variations occurred within the 4th and 5th Tank Battalions, as shown in the tables above. The 3rd Tank Battalion did follow the table of organization, but it retained its old M4A2s, while the other two battalions had new M4A3s.

The flail was based on truck and jeep parts mounted to the front of a former dozer tank. The chains beat the ground and detonated mines. The overall structure remained however vulnerable to mortar and gunfire. The tank was also greatly under powered when the flail was in motion. (NARA via Ed Gilbert).

The rod-like shape of the fuel stream coming out of the muzzle of this flame tank indicates the weapon utilizes thickened fuel rather than liquid. Liquid fuel tends to be consumed immediately as it comes out of the weapon's nozzle thus reducing its effectiveness. The wall of flame created was however considered as having a more important shock and demoralization impact on the enemy. (Sergeant Major Bert Nave)

Before shipping from Hawaii, eight M4A3s were converted by the US Navy Construction Battalions into large-capacity flamethrowers. The flamethrower mechanism was inserted into the cannon of the tank, thereby not modifying the external appearance of the vehicle.

The weapon utilized thickened fuel (napalm), contained in cells located under the turret totaling 290 gallons. This modification significantly increased the tank's weight by 1,500lb (680kgs). Although the turret traverse was limited to 270°, the gun's elevation and depression were not affected. The flame burst had a range of some 140 yards (depending on the fuel's quality), making it a terrible weapon for enemy forces to face. Designated POA-CWS-H1, the flamethrower proved very reliable on Iwo Jima, suffering only minor problems, the most troublesome being fuel leaking into the turret from inside the main gun barrel. To prevent flashbacks, crewmen packed asbestos between the gun barrel and the flamethrower mechanism.

However, towards the end of the battle on Iwo Jima, after days of extensive use, one of the flamethrower tanks deployed with the 5th Battalion caught fire and the tank completely burned out.

Four converted flame tanks were provided to both the 4th and 5th Tank Battalions. In addition, each of these battalions carried 24 E4-5 mechanized flamethrowers to be used by the tank's bow machine gunner, who could either use the standard .30cal machine gun or the flame gun. The fuel and CO_2 cells were located inside the right sponson of the tank and had a capacity of 24 gallons. An additional 24-gallon fuel cell was mounted over the transmission to increase the weapon's capacity. Its range depended on the nature and quality of the fuel: from 25–30 yards with liquid gas to 50–70 yards with thickened fuel, although the latter was rarely available on Iwo Jima. The 3rd Tank Battalion, meanwhile, carried only 13 mechanized flamethrowers but they were an improved model, the E4R2-5R1.

Another modification was undertaken by C Company of the 4th Tank Battalion to cope with minefields. Inspired by the British flail tanks used in Normandy, Gunnery Sergeant Samuel Johnson and Staff Sergeant Ray Shaw built their own flail, using an old tank dozer from which the blade was removed and jeep and truck parts assembled.

Corporal John C. Carey, a flail tank gunner on Iwo Jima, commented: "At the last minute [...] they decided that our tank would be great to have a flail on it. A flail is a couple of barrels out front with chains on them and you raised them up and down to beat the ground for land mines."

Trials were conducted on Hawaii, and after the test vehicle was successfully evaluated a second tank dozer was converted and turned over to A Company. These two vehicles were the only M4A2 diesel tanks taken to Iwo Jima by the 4th Tank Battalion.

TECHNICAL FACTORS

Iwo Jima armor technical characteristics							
	Japanese tanks			American tanks			
Tank model	Type 95 Ha-Go (both early and late production)	Type 97 Chi-Ha (both early and late production)	Type 97 Shinhoto Chi-Ha	M4A2 Sherman (both mid- and late production)	M4A3(75)W Sherman	LVT(A)-4	M3 GMC
Engine	Mitsubishi NVD6 120, 6 cylinders, air-cooled, diesel	Mitsubishi SA 12200VD, V-12 diesel air-cooled	Mitsubishi SA 12200VD, V-12 diesel air-cooled	Twin General Motors 6046, 12 cylinders, water-cooled, diesel	Ford GAA, 8 cylinders, water-cooled, gasoline	Continental W670-9A, 7 cylinders, air-cooled, gasoline	White 160AX, 6 cylinders, water-cooled, gasoline
Armor thickness (hull front)	12mm	25mm	25mm	51mm mid-prod/64mm late prod	64mm	6mm	12mm (cabin front plate)
Weight	7.6 tons	14 tons	15.8 tons	30 tons mid-prod/32 tons late prod	31.5 tons	18.1 tons	9.1 tons
Number of crew	3	4	4–5	5	5	6–7	5
Main armament	Type 94 (37mm) in early model/Type 98 (37mm) in late model*	Type 97 (57mm)	Type 1 (47mm)	M3 (75mm)	M3 (75mm) or converted CB MkI flamethrower	M8 (75mm howitzer)	M1897A4 (75mm)
Secondary armament	2x Type 97s Mgs (7.7mm)	2x Type 97s Mgs (7.7mm)	2x Type 97s Mgs (7.7mm)	3x M1919A4 Mgs (7.62mm) + 1x mechanized flamethrower (optional)	Same as M4A2s. In 5th Tank Bn one of the M1919A4s replaced by one M2 HB (12.7mm)	2x M1919A4 Mgs (7.62mm) + 1x M2 HB Mg (12.7mm)	2x M1919A4 Mgs (7.62mm) + 1x M2 HB Mg (12.7mm)

* Both guns used different ammunition

Japanese antitank weapons

The Japanese started the war in Asia with a very limited number of specific antitank guns (37mm Type 94). Back then, the Japanese doctrine mainly relied on infantry-borne weapons (satchel charges) and on combatant spirit, which was initially believed to be sufficient to overcome any enemy industrial power.

At the battle of Nomonhan (Khalkin Gol) in May 1939, however, the Japanese realized their antitank doctrine was unsuited to modern warfare. Here, insufficient numbers and types of specific tank and antitank guns were judged responsible for the Japanese debacle at the hands of Soviet Union forces.

As a result, a new weapon was designed in 1941 and was to become the most effective antitank weapons in the Japanese arsenal: the Type 1 47mm antitank gun. A version was also developed as a tank gun, and was put in a new turret that equipped the Type 97 Chi-Ha from 1942, giving birth to the Shinhoto

The Type 99 magnetic grenade mine was the most prolific antitank weapon used in the Pacific by the Japanese in WWII. It was fitted with four magnets that were holding the disc of explosive against flat steel surfaces. Its efficiency against US medium tanks was limited but this weapon had a huge psychological impact on American tank crews. (NARA)

Chi-Ha. This was the only real lesson applied by the Japanese from the Khalkin Gol defeat. The antitank doctrine itself had never fully evolved in Japan. By 1945, there were still too few modern antitank weapons in Japanese hands to do without the individual infantry tank-hunter, which remained the backbone of Japanese antitank warfare. A soldier or sailor equipped with explosives was supposed to hurl them at enemy tanks, most often resulting in his own death. The tank-hunters operated in groups of between two and nine men.

Likewise, mines were late in arrival for the forces of Japan. Until the fall of 1944, the Japanese made little use of land mines, since their tactics were based on active defense. The Japanese would instead systematically counterattack to gain time and permit external reinforcements to arrive and help them to regain control of lost territory. The lack of a specially designed antitank land mine led the Japanese to develop improvised explosive devices using aerial bombs, antiboat mines, clusters of explosives, and even designing their own explosives in the field.

Tank and antitank guns

On Iwo Jima, about 40 Type 1 47mm antitank guns equipped the island's five independent antitank battalions. Theoretically, each of these battalions comprised 12 47mm antitank guns. Nevertheless, not enough Type 1s were available so some 20 Type 94 37mm antitank guns were used as a stopgap measure. Furthermore, mortars, rockets, antiaircraft, antiboat, and artillery guns would be turned into antitank weapons, though they were not initially designed for the purpose. The most efficient converted weapon against American tanks appeared to be the Type 90 75mm field gun.

Most artillery pieces and antitank guns were located underground, with alternate positions of fire. Terrain was extensively utilized by the Japanese to conceal weapons. Every attempt was made to canalize enemy tanks onto narrow – mined – routes, covered with machine guns and several guns.

Since terrain was naturally not favorable to tanks, and in order to increase the island's defensive fire power, LtCol Nishi ordered his men to dig emplacements into the ground for tanks to disguise their silhouette. Some were converted into pillboxes and were entirely buried, with only the turret protruding from the ground. Other emplacements were open on one side, permitting the tank to leave the revetment. Caves were also carved into hillsides to protect tanks from American shellfire. There were more emplacements than tanks, allowing crewmen to move from one emplacement to another during the fighting. This was intended to avoid detection and increase confusion within enemy ranks.

Instead of spreading his small armored contingent all around the island, Nishi decided to concentrate them around the second airfield.

Originally, the 26th Tank Regiment's infantry company was trained to ride on tanks to attack enemy lines. However, the new Japanese defense-

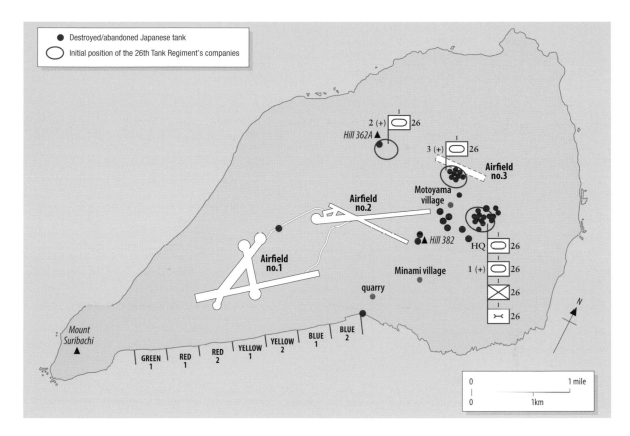

● Destroyed/abandoned Japanese tank

⬭ Initial position of the 26th Tank Regiment's companies

in-depth plan deployed infantry, engineers, and mechanics as tank-hunters equipped with light weapons (rifles, grenades, and machine guns) and a variety of explosives to be used against American tanks.

The Japanese defenders buried some of their tanks into the ground to reduce their silhouette and make them difficult to locate to enemy ground troops. This Type 97 Chi-Ha belonged to the 2nd Company and was located near Hill 362A. It was knocked out on D+8 by Shermans of B Company 5th Tank Battalion. (NARA)

Japanese guns technical data and capabilities

Type of weapon	Model (caliber)	Weight	Muzzle velocity (if applicable)	Effectiveness against US tanks
Antitank gun	Type 94 (37mm)	327kg	2,327ft/sec (AP round)	AP round: penetrated 46mm of rolled steel armor-plate at 119 yards "In some instances, it has penetrated the armor on the turret [and sides] of the US medium tank M4"
Antitank gun	Type 1 (47mm)	753kg	2,720ft/sec (AP round)	AP round: (angle of incidence <20°) 800 yards and below: penetrated hull sides and turret of M4 Ricochet when angle of incidence >20° Cannot penetrate front slope even at short ranges (200 yards)
Tank gun	Type 1 (47mm)	166kg	2,650ft/sec (AP round)	AP round (angle of incidence: 0°): 350 yards: penetrates 2¼in. of turret armor (M4) 500 yards: penetrates 3¼in. of turret armor (M4)*
Tank gun	Type 94 (37mm)	138kg	1,880ft/sec (AP round)	AP round: $1^2/_5$in. at 300 yards
Tank gun	Type 98 (37mm)	Unknown	2,200ft/sec (nature of round unknown, probably HE)	AP round: 2in. at 100 yards (homogeneous steel)
Tank gun	Type 97 (57mm)	128kg (tube only)	1,260ft/sec (estimated)	AP round: capable of penetrating the sponsons of a Sherman at close ranges (<200 yards)
Field gun	Type 90 (75mm)	1,597kg	2,230ft/sec (HE shell)	AP round: 250 yards: penetrates 3½in. 500 yards: penetrates 3.3in. Capable of penetrating Sherman armor anywhere except front slope

*M4 turret armor is 2¼in. thick. Here, the test round penetrated one side of the turret and dug another 1in. deep hole on the opposite turret wall

Infantry-borne weapons

The most commonly used explosives were the Type 99 magnetic grenade-mine and the Type 93 "tape measure" mine. Though they were not powerful enough to penetrate the sides of a Sherman tank, they played a major psychological role against tank crews, especially the Type 99. These mines were often used in clusters to increase their efficiency.

A more elaborate hollow-charge mine was used on Iwo Jima for the first time. The Type 3 Model B conical hand-thrown mine was efficient when placed against tank sides, but necessitated the user to keep the explosive in place until it detonated.

Two hollow-charge rifle grenades were also encountered: the 30mm and 40mm Type 2, both capable of penetrating the side and turret armor plates of a Sherman.

Locally made explosives, placed in wooden boxes and carried by soldiers, were also used. Though they had no direct antitank roles, standard and frangible hand-grenades and Molotov cocktails were extensively used to literally "blind" tank crews and permit tank-destroyer units to swarm immobile vehicles with more effective explosives.

The Japanese often combined explosives to increase their efficiency. Here, two Type 93 "tape measure" mines were strapped to a stick to facilitate access to the suspension system of American tanks. (NARA)

Contrary to what is commonly believed, the lunge mine was not used by the Japanese on Iwo Jima.

The table below lists the most commonly used infantry-borne explosives on Iwo Jima.

Japanese infantry-borne explosives technical data and capabilities		
Model	Quantity of explosive	Capabilities
Type 99 magnetic grenade-mine	0.5kg	Can penetrate 20mm of rolled steel armor (damage engine); cannot penetrate 35mm
Type 93 "Tape-measure" mine	0.9kg	Can break a track
Type 3 Model B conical hand-thrown mine	0.6kg	Can penetrate Sherman sponsons, except when equipped with field-expedient armor
Type 2 rifle grenade (30mm)	0.05kg	Penetrates 2½in. of Sherman turret armor at 50 yards

Land mines

Iwo Jima was the first battle in which Japanese forces made extensive use of minefields. They were strategically located on avenues of approach and were usually covered by light or heavy guns, rendering their removal difficult. Typically, mines would be lain in staggered rows and spaced from seven to 25 paces apart. Another technique was to sporadically mine avenues through which American tanks had already been operating. By so doing, when they returned the next day, the tankers would not suspect to find mines in their old tracks.

Iwo Jima would see the first use of the Type 3 pottery or terracotta land mine. However, the lack of specially designed antitank mines led the Japanese to utilize a wide variety of explosives, as shown in the table below. It was common to combine explosives to improve results against American armor, for example taping a yardstick mine to an aerial bomb or shell. It is worth mentioning that, as with lunge mines, torpedo warheads were not utilized on Iwo Jima.

Japanese mines technical data and capabilities		
Model	Quantity of explosive	Capabilities
Type 2 two-horn hemispherical, antiboat	18kg	Can destroy Sherman suspension system
Type 1 single-horn conical, antiboat	9kg	Can destroy Sherman suspension system
Yardstick or Bo-Jirai, anti-vehicles	2.7kg	Can break a track
Type 3 Model A terracotta, antitank	3kg	Can destroy Sherman suspension system
Type 3 Model B wooden box, antitank	2kg	Probably can destroy suspension system
Type 94 63kg aerial bomb	20kg	Can destroy Sherman suspension system
Type 92 250kg aerial bomb	107kg	Can destroy a Sherman tank
Type 2 depth-charge, antiboat	113kg	Can destroy a Sherman tank

USMC improvised tank armor

The early campaigns in the Solomon Islands had revealed that the Japanese antitank doctrine mostly relayed on infantry-borne weapons, and particularly the Type 99 magnetic grenade-mine. The explosive was effective to some extent when positioned in the suspension system or on the hull sides, rear, and top of the M2 and M3 light tanks. But beyond the actual damage caused, an important psychological impact was created around the weapon

RIGHT
The Type 3 terracotta mine was an effective antitank mine: it was capable of disabling an M4 Sherman by breaking its suspension system. Its main body was made of clay, hence its name, rendering its detection difficult. (NMPW)

FAR RIGHT
Aerial bombs were disposed on the landing beaches, airfields, and wide routes and were intended to stop armored vehicles' progress. The large 250kg ones were capable of destroying a Sherman while the smaller 63kg bombs would only destroy the suspension system. (NARA)

by American tank crews. As a result, the magnetic mine remained feared by tank personnel until very late in the war, though its effectiveness against the Sherman was very limited.

The first countermeasure the Marines developed against the Type 99 was improvised by the 3rd Tank Battalion on Bougainville in November 1943. Here, crew members covered the sides of their M3A1s with canvas to prevent the Type 99 magnets from sticking to the vertical surfaces of the vehicles. Although the device worked well, the dense vegetation encountered tended to damage the canvas and the unit did not reconduct the experiment in future operations.

One of the most iconic Marine Corps tank modifications was first used in early 1944 prior to the Marshall Islands campaign. Simultaneously, C Company of the 4th Tank Battalion and the 2nd Separate Tank Company, both equipped with M4A2 medium tanks, decided to place wood boards on the sides of their vehicles to deflect magnetic mines. In C Company, the modification was undertaken while en route to the twin islands of Roi-Namur:

The crews of the medium tanks, while aboard ship, placed a two inch layer of lumber around the tanks, retaining a two inch airspace between the lumber

B

1. AFLAMO: M4A3 75(W), FLAME TANK, 2ND PLATOON, A COMPANY, 4TH TANK BATTALION
Converted flamethrower tanks were externally identical to traditional gun tanks. This prevented the Japanese from identifying specialized vehicles but had the disadvantage of confusing friendly infantry, which had difficulty in recognizing flame tanks. This tank survived the Iwo Jima campaign and was turned over to the 3rd Tank Battalion when the 4th Tank Battalion left the island.

2. M4A3 75(W), GUN TANK, 1ST PLATOON, A COMPANY, 5TH TANK BATTALION
Geometric figures were used by the 5th Tank Battalion to indicate the company to which the tank belonged. A square stood for A Company, a circle for B Company, and a diamond for C Company. The two digits numbers give the platoon and position of the tank. This tank was the lowest-ranking tank of 1st Platoon and was lost east of Suribachi, after running over a mine around D+2. The tank was definitively destroyed by friendly fire after the Japanese occupied it. It was equipped with an E-4-5 flamethrower.

1

2

62

The first designed field protection against magnetic mines consisted in sticking canvas with rubber cement to the sponsons of tanks. Here is an example in use on Eniwetok in 1944 on a Sherman belonging to the 2nd Separate Tank Company. (NARA)

and the armor plate. This was accomplished by welding strips of two inch angle iron to the sides of the tanks and bolting two-by-twelve planks to the angle iron.

The 2nd Separate Tank Company modified its tanks in early January while in Hawaii:

We put mesh wire on top [of the tank hull] about two inches off the hull, secured to iron braces, and we had lumber on some tank sides, and rubber cement and canvas on others.

In the case of C Company, which saw combat first, the modifications were of no use since no Japanese antitank weapons were encountered. However, the company's Commanding Officer, Captain Robert M. Neiman, wrote that: "It is believed that this lumber and air space would be sufficient to cause A.P.-H.E. [Armor Piercing High Explosive] shells to detonate before penetrating the tanks' armor plate. Thus, the lumber could serve two useful functions".[3]

After the fight on Eniwetok, the 2nd Separate Tank Company concluded that, "All of these [modifications] appeared effective, but the canvas ripped off against trees; and the engine grille should have a raised netting for protection." But the short and violent action on the tiny atoll, during which Japanese soldiers and sailors used magnetic mines, proved that "these mines were not effective against side armor [of the medium tanks]". They could, however, damage an engine if placed on top of the grille.

Antitank guns were not encountered during these two operations, but were faced by Marine tank crews on Guadalcanal, New Georgia, and Tarawa. Their effect on light and medium tanks were not negligible. On Tarawa, the 37mm Type 94 and the 75mm Type 88 guns were capable of penetrating the side armor of an M4 at close ranges. The Japanese,

3   The idea of putting wood boards on the sides of tanks was given to Neiman by 1st Lt Leo B. Case who fought on Guadalcanal in August 1942 with A Company, 1st Tank Battalion.

however, deployed few antitank guns, so they were yet to be considered as an important threat by the US Marine tankers. The situation was identical with landmines: they were seldom encountered in the early stages of the war in the Pacific.

That would change with the Marianas and Palau operations in 1944.

The battles for Saipan and Tinian in June and July 1944 proved to be the most influential campaigns as to the nature of the modifications the Marine tankers would develop on their tanks.

Of the two tank battalions deployed (the 2nd and 4th), the old C Company, 4th Tank Battalion, was the only unit to attach lumber to the sides of its tanks, as it did on Roi-Namur. In addition, plywood boards cut to the shape of the glacis were put on the front of each tank, while sandbags were piled on top of the engine decks and an armored cover was welded on top of the tank commander's periscope. As it turned out, the Japanese made extensive use of magnetic mines in these battles. In most cases, the Japanese aimed at the flat surfaces of the tanks, disabling engines, cracking fuel tanks, and breaking periscopes. On two occasions, magnetic mines placed on top of the hatches of tanks from the 4th Battalion killed the crewman underneath.

After the campaign, the 4th Tank Battalion's commanding officer recommended, "That all tanks have all possible hull armor covered with one inch lumber with at least one inch air space between the lumber and the hull. [...] The addition of lumber to the tank hulls is apparently no additional fire hazard."

First Lieutenant Walter H. Crumps of B Company, 4th Tank Battalion, recommended: "Some sort of air space should be developed above the tank's hull. This could be accomplished by the use of chicken wire, metal strips or wood. This space would greatly reduce the shock of a magnetic AT mine explosion."

The Japanese Type 88 75mm antiaircraft gun was used as an antitank weapon and was responsible for the loss of several tanks and crewmen. In C Company, 4th Tank Battalion, one M4A2 was knocked out by such a weapon on Saipan: the 75mm round broke the lumber and penetrated inside the crew compartment, killing the driver instantly.

The Type 1 47mm antitank gun was rarely encountered. Several tanks were hit by long-range fire with such weapons on the front slope and turret, but they caused no damage.

C Company, 4th Tank Battalion, ran into another situation showing the need to reinforce protection on their tanks. On 31 July 1944, during mopping-up operations on Tinian, two tanks were fired at by a 47mm antitank gun, hidden some 30 yards away inside a concrete emplacement. Major Robert M. Neiman described the wounds sustained by two of the unit's tanks:

The first tank to be hit received seven hits, one of which penetrated the turret and the balance of which

C Company 4th Tank Battalion was the first unit to make wide use of field expedient armor consisting of 2x12in. wooden planks. Note the plywood board on the front armor slope used to deflect magnetic mines and the armored cover above the tank commander's periscope. Marianas Islands, mid-1944. (NARA)

failed to come completely through. [...] The other tank received six hits, three of which were on the side below the turret and all three of those hits penetrated. On the second tank, one projectile entered [the] left fuel tank and caused the fuel to leak out but failed to set the diesel oil on fire. The other two projectiles that penetrated the second tank entered the fighting compartment, wounding the loader, tank commander, and gunner. One of the projectiles that entered the fighting compartment hit and severed two HE shells in the ammunition racks, the other projectile hit and cut off the nose of a smoke shell and continued on to hit and destroy a radio junction box.

Sergeant Bert R. Nave was in the second tank to be hit. He described the situation of the panicked crew:

One round entered [the turret] and ricocheted around and took all of the fuses off [of] the ammunition. They were thermal shells with a fuse that stuck way up. So when the round clipped off all the fuses, we were in a hurry to get them out of the tank – one of them could have set all the others off.

The enemy gun was finally located and silenced by the two crippled but still-running M4s.

Land mines were encountered during the final phase of the Saipan operation and on Tinian. On Saipan, such a late disposal of mines was due to the fact that the Japanese expected external support from troops, ships, or planes that would help them repel the American landing. When the Japanese realized the expected support would not be coming, they hastily began laying minefields, most of which were rapidly discovered by American troops. Indeed, the Japanese lacked knowledge in laying and concealing mines: in many instances, detonators were missing or not properly plugged into the explosive. Nevertheless, they did cause tanks and infantry to slow down their progress, it being time consuming for engineers to remove all the devices.

Most of these were traditional mines ("tape measure", horned, or yard stick mines), but some improvised devices were also encountered. The most commonly used was a 63kg aerial bomb, buried fuse-up with a standard mine used as a detonator. Their effects on tanks could be devastating.

On Guam, similar defensive techniques were employed by the Japanese. The Tank Company of the 22nd Marines (the former 2nd Separate Tank Company) again used wooden boards bolted on U-shaped bars welded to the

C

1. M3 GUN MOTOR CARRIAGE, WEAPONS COMPANY, 27TH MARINES, 5TH MARINE DIVISION

Half-tracks' paint scheme varied widely on Iwo Jima. Some M3s were finished in overall olive drab while others, such as this vehicle, had elaborate multicolor camouflage paint. Occasionally, names were added on the sides of the half-tracks. As shown here, assault vehicles were fitted with chains on the front wheels to increase traction in the soft volcanic ash.

2. M4A2 (MID), DOZER TANK, HQ PLATOON, C COMPANY, 3RD TANK BATTALION

By early 1944, the 3rd Tank Battalion was reorganized and rebuilt around Marines from the I Corps Tank Battalion (medium). Except for one company which fought on Tarawa, the remainder of the unit had experience with the M4A2 and unused vehicles. The old D Company, I Corps Tank Battalion (medium), became C Company, 3rd Tanks, but retained names starting with the letter "D." The former battalion's symbol, an elephant, was retained and could be seen on several tanks on Iwo Jima. The two digits on the turret indicate the platoon and the vehicle's position within it.

DESTROYER

54

DOZER

1

2

This 5th Tank Battalion Sherman sports a wide variety of modifications intended to increase tank crew chances of survival. These modifications consisted in lumber bolted to the sponsons and suspension system, track blocs welded on the turret sides and spikes welded on the hatches and periscopes. Several tank crews within the 5th Tank Battalion added saw-toothed steel sheets on the edges of the sponson's lumber to prevent Japanese soldiers from grabbing the plank sides and climb on the vehicles. (MCHD)

sides of some of its vehicles, as well as chicken-wire on the flat surface of the hull. But the wood protection and chicken-wire proved to be unsatisfactory: the former did not resist antitank gunfire, while the latter was not solid enough to survive extensive use in densely vegetated areas.

The Tank Company of the 4th Marines, meanwhile, welded steel plate kits on the turret and on the sponsons, where the ammunition was stored. The 3rd Tank Battalion did not conduct any pre-invasion modifications. A few tank crews welded tank tracks on the sponsons and turret in the field, but their usefulness was not attested during the fighting.

In the summer of 1944, the 1st Tank Battalion decided to generalize the employment of tank tracks as additional protection for tanks:

> Experimentation was carried out to determine the effectiveness of spaced armor in defeating the Japanese anti-tank grenade which penetrated our medium tank turrets in previous operations [Cape Gloucester]. These tests indicated [steel] tank tracks to be the most effective. With the track guides toward the armor face, both the bazooka and U.S. Anti-Tank Rifle Grenade failed to penetrate the armor behind the interrupted grouser type tank track.

Thus, eight track blocks were welded on either side of the tank turrets. The Peleliu operation showed the value of such field-expedient decisions by offering protection from small-caliber gun rounds and various types of infantry-borne explosives.

In addition, the 1st Tank Battalion welded metal plates on the holes of the tanks' wheels to prevent Japanese soldiers from throwing rifles or crowbars into the wheels and thereby immobilizing the vehicles. In the first Marine tank engagements, several light tanks were reportedly immobilized by such methods. In actuality, natural causes had initially been responsible for disabling the vehicles and the Japanese intended to further immobilize the tanks by using such means. Although metal bars and rifle barrels inserted into road wheels were actually easily broken by a moving light or medium tank, the myth persisted within many Marine tank units.[4]

Modifications for Iwo Jima

Prior to Iwo Jima, the three Marine tank battalions designated to support the assault undertook a more or less elaborate series of modifications on their tanks to protect against Japanese antitank weapons.

The 3rd Tank Battalion, despite experience gained in other battles, did not make any extensive modification to its vehicles. The unit retained its old M4A2s, to which extra armor plates were welded. These plates were concentrated on the turret and sponsons to increase crew and ammunition protection.

The 4th and 5th Tank Battalions, however, did conduct a series of important modifications to their tanks.

Though the newly formed 5th Tank Battalion had not yet experienced combat, it benefited from other units' experience. The fact that both the 4th and 5th Divisions were stationed on Hawaii from late 1944 probably played a major role in the decision by the 5th Tank Battalion to use extra armor.

Prior to the assault on Iwo Jima, four types of additional armor were designed and put on tank sponsons:

This view of a modified M4A3 shows the casing formed by the added wood on the sides of this 4th Tank Battalion vehicle. Contrarily to what is commonly accepted, the gap between the wood and steel plate was not systematically filled with concrete. Most of the time, the gap was left empty. This particular vehicle is using plywood as anti-magnetic mine protection. (Author's collection)

- Lumber: oak planks covered the sides of the tanks, with a 2–4in.-wide airspace between the hull and lumber. This was the most commonly used configuration by both the 4th and 5th Tank Battalions and was intended to deflect magnetic mines. The lack of available material resulted in B Company, 4th Tank Battalion, using soft pine planks instead of oak.
- Plywood: this was a less common feature. It was also designed to prevent magnetic mines from sticking to the tanks' sides. Like with the modification above, a 3in. airspace was left between the board and the hull to absorb the energy delivered by the explosion of ordinance. This method was mostly employed by A Company, 4th Tank Battalion.
- Lumber with reinforced concrete: the 3½in. airspace between the hull and the wood was filled with concrete, intermingled with rods, heavy mesh, and rebar (reinforcing steel bars). This modification was designed and only used by C Company, 4th Tank Battalion, being intended to improve protection against antitank guns. A similar variant was observed on several vehicles from A Company, 4th Tank Battalion, but used plywood instead of lumber.
- Corrugated steel plate: metal sheets were cut to the shape of the sponson and bolted to angled iron cleats, leaving a 4in.-wide gap. Sometimes it was doubled with wood or plywood panels, and in at least one case the gap was filled with concrete. This modification was limited to B Company, 5th Tank Battalion.

---

4   Measure already undertaken by the 1st Tank Battalion for the New Britain Campaign in December 1943.

RIGHT
This is another example of field expedient armor on this A Company 4th Tank Battalion vehicle on Iwo Jima. Three sections of plywood filled with 3½in. thick concrete were bolted on brackets welded to the sponsons. The wood/concrete panels were removable. (Author's collection)

FAR RIGHT
These vehicles belonged to C Company 4th Tank Battalion and show the most advanced field modifications used on tanks on Iwo Jima. Lumber, steel, and concrete protected the sides against projectiles, while cages protected the hatches against hand-placed explosives. Track-blocks were welded around the turret and front slope to protect against the same threats. (MCHD)

Tanks of both battalions that were fitted with a mechanized flamethrower received an additional armor plate directly welded to the hull's right front half to increase protection around the fuel cell stored in the sponson.

Tank hatches were also protected with several materials to prevent explosives from being employed on these vulnerable spots. The three companies in the 4th Tank Battalion, for example, welded heavy mesh to create a cage above the periscopes and hatches.

A Company, 5th Tank Battalion, welded penny nails points up at 2in. intervals on and around the hatches, periscopes, and air intakes. C Company conducted the same effort on turret hatches, but a lack of materials led them to use chicken wire attached to a frame to create a cage above the hull's hatches. B Company also used chicken wire, but in some cases it was substituted by pierced steel plates.

In addition, most tanks received track blocks (made from rubber or steel) spot-welded around the turret and on the glacis for protection against small-caliber rounds and magnetic mines. Sandbags were also piled on the hull's flat surfaces.

The ultimate modification consisted in covering the tank bogies with a skirt of planks to prevent the Japanese from throwing satchel charges into the tank suspension system. This modification was undertaken only within the 5th Tank Battalion.

D

1. M4A3 75(W), GUN TANK, 4TH PLATOON, B COMPANY, 4TH TANK BATTALION

B Company extensively used camouflage on its tanks. It comprised three or four colors: light and dark olive drab, red earth, and sand. Other than the vehicle's name and number, markings included the UNIS (Unit Numerical Identification System), which was frequently painted on B Company tanks. The half-disc indicated the 4th Division, "9" stood for "Tanks," and "13" for "Company B." The tank was named *Betty* because "it sounds All-American," according to its tank commander, Sergeant Raymond W. Pair.

2. M4A3 75(W), GUN TANK, 2ND PLATOON, B COMPANY, 5TH TANK BATTALION

The use of corrugated steel plates was unique to B Company, 5th Tank Battalion. To increase magnetic mine deflection, several tank crews painted over the plates and sand-sprayed the wet paint. In most cases, the space between the hull armor plate and the false side was left empty. In this particular case, concrete was poured into the gap. The paint scheme consisted of large light brown and olive drab splotches.

1

2

LVT(A)-4s of A Company, 2nd Armored Amphibians Battalion are crossing the line of departure on D-Day. This company is heading for Blue Beach 1. Note the field-made gun-shield for the turret mounted .50cal machine gun. (MCHD)

Amphibious tanks

The LVT(A)-4s from the 2nd Armored Amphibian Battalion were also modified following experience gained in the Marianas operation. Because the ¼in.-thick armor of the LVT was not sufficient to withstand even shell fragments or small-arms fire, factory-made armor plate kits were adapted to the front and sides of the vehicles while the unit was stationed in Saipan prior to Iwo Jima. The added weight from the bow plate (½in.) and side plates (¼in.) did not alter the seaworthiness of the vehicles.

A ½in.-thick 18in.x24in. shield was also designed to protect the tank commander when he manned the turret-mounted .50cal machine gun.

In most cases, these extra armor plates proved sufficient to stop shrapnel and small-arms fire from penetrating the amphibious tanks.

ARMORED WARFARE ON IWO JIMA

Amphibious tanks

The first US armored vehicles to hit the beach on Iwo Jima on the morning of February 19, 1945 were the LVT(A)-4s of the 2nd Armored Amphibian Battalion.

Though the amphibians drew sporadic shell fire as they approached the shoreline, the threat remained only moderate. Greater trouble was encountered when the vehicles hit the beach: the loose volcanic ash did not permit the tracks to grip on the soil, resulting in poor traction. Even worse, the terraces were too steep for the amphibious tanks to reach the flat terrain. As a result, only four vehicles (three from A Company and one from B Company) succeeded in reaching the second terrace.

The other vehicles simply bogged down in the sand. Staying on the shoreline was impossible: the LVT(A)-4s' field of fire was masked by the terraces, and the arriving infantry from the assault waves rendered fire

75mm half-tracks were used to some extent in mop-up operations in northern Iwo Jima. They were mainly used as direct fire weapons as shown here. This section of M3 GMCs is firing point blank on a Japanese pillbox. (MCHD)

missions even more hazardous. As a consequence, many LVT(A)s returned to the water to fire on targets throughout the day.

By mid-morning, Japanese artillery and mortar fire increased on the overcrowded beaches, resulting in high vehicle losses. Some 22 LVT(A)-4s were put out of action in the vicinity of the landing beaches.

During the remainder of the battle, operational armored amphibians stayed on or around the landing beaches and provided beachhead protection.

75mm half-tracks

The LCMs (landing craft mechanized) transporting the 75mm half-tracks arrived with the last waves of infantry, but the M3s faced the same problems as the LVT(A)s.

The volcanic ash and sand terraces immediately hampered their move off of the beach. A good number of vehicles, however, managed to exit the beaches and positioned themselves to fire on the high ground overlooking the shore.

Half-tracks saw only limited use on Iwo Jima. The M3s' open top crew compartment, thin armor, narrow tracks, and mechanical weaknesses made them very vulnerable to both the terrain and Japanese action. The tank destroyer's role of the half-track was not used since no Japanese tanks were encountered by any of them.

When close infantry support was needed, tanks were generally preferred since they were more protected and could also go where half-tracks could.

The only advantage of the 75mm half-tracks over the tanks were their main weapon's accuracy. Thus, the M3 was extensively used in mop-up operations, particularly in the northern part of the island. It was also common for 75mm half-tracks to act in support of tank formations to increase their firepower. The presence of the half-tracks among tank formations permitted the provision of the infantry with continuous gunfire support, especially when tanks had to leave the front line for ammunition resupply.

Tanks
The landing and battle for airfield No. 1
On Iwo Jima, traditional tank tactics and the use of armor as close infantry

LSM 141 is seen discharging tanks of B Company 5th Tank Battalion on Iwo Jima on D-Day. The considerable weight of the dozer blade lead this vehicle to bog down in the soft volcanic ash a few yards away from the shore. C Company landed a few hours before and two of its tanks can be seen disabled on the right, after running over mines. (MCHD)

Sergeant Charles H. Saulmon inspects the damages sustained by his tank after running over a mine near Yellow Beach 2. The "Cairo" was the first tank out of LSM 126. The 2nd Platoon tanks in C Company, 4th Tank Battalion were all named after capital cities: "Cairo," "Calcutta," and "Capetown". (NARA)

support weapons materialized on rare occasions due to the nature of the terrain and Japanese defenses. The American tank company structure was used as a whole only during the landing on D-Day and for the battles on the airfields which permitted the use of large tank formations.

Tanks were not landed at prearranged schedules, but instead came ashore at the request of the regimental landing team commanders. This was intended to give time for tank reconnaissance personnel to search the most favorable spots to land the tanks and avoid unnecessary congestion on the beach.

On Iwo Jima, assault tank battalions faced extremely difficult landing conditions due to several factors. First, the nature of the beaches themselves, made of soft volcanic ash, were unsuited to most vehicles. In most places, the beach comprised successive terraces, more or less steep, forming a natural tank barrier. Except on rare parts of the beaches, tanks were unable to negotiate loose volcanic ash, and openings in the terraces had to be made by wide-tracked bulldozers.

The second difficulty was inherent to the tactic of bringing in armored support well after the first waves of infantry. With the battle raging all along the beaches, tanks faced overcrowded terrain as soon as the landing ship ramps were downed. Scattered supplies and Marines were among the obstacles that contributed to the slowness of tank progress off of the beaches.

In addition, minefields were located on or immediately beyond most beaches. Although engineers cleared and marked safe routes for tanks, the removal of mines was not an exact science and columns of tanks exiting the beaches were delayed by the remaining unmoved mines.

The experience of tanks from 2nd and 3rd Platoon, C Company, 4th Tank Battalion, which landed on Yellow Beach One from LSM 126, illustrates the chaos of the landing and the difficulty to reach the high ground beyond the beaches. As the ship approached the beach, it was taken under fire from the guns and mortars located on Mount Suribachi to the left and the high ground located in front and to the right of the landing site.

E

1. M4A2 (LATE), FLAIL TANK, HQ PLATOON, C COMPANY, 4TH TANK BATTALION

This tank was put out of action on D-Day by Japanese mortar fire on airfield No. 1. The flail device was damaged beyond use, but the M4A2 was later repaired and used by its crew until it ran over a mine in late March 1945. It was thereafter turned over to the 3rd Tank Battalion. Its twin in A Company shared a similar fate.

2. M32B3, HQ PLATOON, C COMPANY, 4TH TANK BATTALION

The recovery vehicles were indispensable for mechanics to keep 60 percent of the tanks operational during the battle for Iwo Jima. Only eight were available. Contrary to the other companies within the 4th Tank Battalion, C Company did not use camouflage paint on its tanks and retained an overall dark olive drab. The name and number were usually painted in yellow, though white paint was occasionally employed. The use of UNIS markings is rather unusual for C Company.

1

34
CYANIDE

2

This picture taken on D-Day shows a column of tanks from A Company, 4th Tank Battalion coming off the Blue Beaches. In the center, the company flail tank is visible a few minutes before it was knocked out by Japanese fire. (MCHD)

When the bow gate of the LSM opened, its six M4A3s slugged out. After several minutes spent immobile, the situation aboard ship was becoming untenable. Sergeant Bert R. Nave, in the tank dubbed "Cracker," recalled: "I was the last tank off of the LSM. You could see shots going right through from one side to the other. They were really laying it into the LSM. They turned everything loose."

Upon reaching the flat terrain above the terraces, the three 2nd Platoon tanks broke their tracks: two to mines, the other to the soft volcanic ash.

The 3rd Platoon vehicles fared a little better, only the platoon leader's tank hitting a mine and breaking a track.

Platoon Sergeant Joe Bruno and Sergeant Nave were more successful. Nave recalled:

I don't know how we managed to get up there [to the airfield] because they had anti-boat mines [Type 98] laid out all over the place. You could see the horns of these things sticking out of the ground.

We pulled up to a road, and then there was a swale [drainage ditch] and then there was the airfield. Our turrets could look over the swale and we had a full vision of the airfield. That was when the nips left the beaches and were all moving across the airfield. I don't know how many we wiped out. It was a turkey shoot.

Soon, they were joined by elements of the 1st Battalion, 23rd Marines (1/23 Marines) and "went up onto the airfield," recalled Nave. "I could see Joe's tank at the other end, south of us, coming up about the same time we did. He was closer to Mount Suribashi [*sic*]."

They were joined in the melee by other Shermans, including the C Company flail tank. Corporal John C. Carey, who was gunning for Sergeant James R. Haddix in the modified Sherman, recalled:

We're on the plane field and we could see all the fighting going on. [After] about three or four minutes a big gun started shooting at us. I guess he was 155mm gun.[5] And his first shot hit us point blank and just ripped that whole damn dumb flail off of the front of our tank! Now we were just a tank again: we could fight!

But we didn't last long the first day: they blew our tracks off ... We didn't get a chance to really do any damage the first day.

The next day, C Company provided 11 operational tanks, which were divided into three reinforced platoons to support the assault of the 23rd Marines on airfield No. 1. Tanks deployed ahead of the riflemen, shooting at all suspicious targets. At first, no return fire was observed. After a few minutes of progress, heavy mortar rounds began falling among the Marines.

5   No such pieces were present in this area. Large-caliber coastal defense guns were located on the heights. The incoming fire was most likely heavy mortar bombs, as suggested by the tank commander, James R. Haddix.

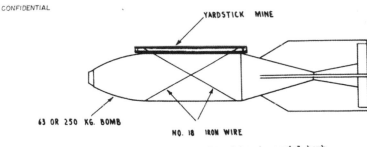

CONFIDENTIAL

YARDSTICK MINE

63 OR 250 KG. BOMB

NO. 18 IRON WIRE

Yardstick mine employed to detonate aerial bomb.

An engineer sketch of an aerial bomb converted to a landmine, using a yardstick mine as a detonator. Sgt Joe Bruno ran over one such improvised explosive device on Airfield No. 1. (NARA)

Japanese gunners opened fire from all sides, aiming their weapons at exposed targets. Realizing the potential tank terrain represented by the airfield, the Japanese strategically concealed mines on it. Bert Nave stated: "The next day they switched Joe and I. I was to go where Joe had been [the previous day]. I told Joe to follow my tracks through the minefield and he did. He ran over a 500pound mine [Type 92]."

In the tank named *Cleaver*, Sergeant Joe Bruno was guiding his driver:

I just told my driver to make a right turn and get down to the runway. And Christ, I did not remember anything after that except coming to and looking over and seeing a tank upside down with its turret gone saying "Christ! Who in the hell's tank is that?" And unfortunately it happened to be mine.

The tank had run over a yardstick mine attached to a 250kg aerial bomb. In detonating, the yardstick mine set off the aerial bomb and the huge explosion threw the 35-ton Sherman in the air, blowing the turret clean off the hull. Miraculously, Bruno and his gunner, though both badly injured, managed to survive the terrific explosion. The other crewmen died.

Sergeant Parker in "Cyuzie" also hit an improvised mine, but fortunately for the crew, only the yardstick mine exploded, breaking the tank's right-hand track but failing to ignite the aerial bomb. All five crew members made it out safely.

Despite casualties in tanks and men, the attack continued, facing stronger opposition as the afternoon wore on. Tank-infantry coordination resulted

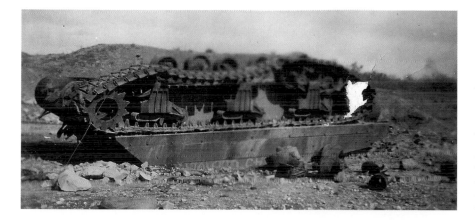

The wreck of "Cleaver", the M4A3 commanded by Platoon Sergeant Joe Bruno on Iwo Jima after it ran over an aerial bomb. The turret was blown off the hull and fell several yards away. Two crewmen eventually survived the terrific explosion. (From the collection of Sergeant Major Bert Nave)

Tank-infantry telephones were fitted to the rear of each vehicle for infantry to designate targets to the tank crew. As shown in the picture, the use of the telephone increased infantrymen's vulnerability. The two antennas on the turret of this tank indicate it was equipped with an SCR-300 radio, a model also in use by the infantry. This permitted better and safer communication between tanks and infantry. It was preferred to the telephone but only one tank per platoon was equipped with an SCR-300. (NARA)

in the reduction of numerous pillboxes, bunkers, and other Japanese pockets of resistance. Using the telephone located to the rear of each tank, infantrymen directed the tank fire directly onto Japanese emplacements. The process was, however, hazardous for the men following the tanks. The 23rd Marines' action report stated that "The mere appearance of a tank forward with the infantry during the attack resulted in heavy artillery and mortar fire being directed at the vehicles and consequently into the lines of the advancing infantry, causing heavy casualties."

Heavy mortar fire was now accurately directed on the slowly progressing Marines, and one such round knocked out Nave's tank. He recalled:

> About that time something [big] hit my tank and blew the hatches off and knocked the turret off the turret ring so it was kind of teetering. [...] We didn't have the periscopes but it was still running. We managed to steer it back to the command post. That was the end of my tank.

During the Marianas operation, friendly tanks were cherished and their sight on the battlefield was synonymous with protection for the exposed riflemen. However, this feeling of safety vanished in the first few days of the battle for Iwo Jima. Consequently, it became common for infantry to order the tanks to withdraw to permit a "safer" attack for troops on the ground.

Unsuitable terrain and minefields also prevented tanks from providing further assistance to infantry on the northern and eastern ends of the airfield. While the remainder of the airfield was captured by infantry, tanks reduced bypassed Japanese pockets of resistance. Infantry and tanks, however, then had to give up hard-gained terrain for the night and retreat to a more defensible perimeter.

Type 1 47mm antitank gun vs field-expedient armor

The terrain between the first two airfields became the proving ground for the concrete-steel-lumber modification of the Shermans of C Company, 4th Tank Battalion.

The area was covered by a multitude of artillery and antitank weapons, including the Type 1 47mm antitank gun. Tanks were forced to move on a narrow mined road, where engineers worked to remove the explosives under constant enemy fire. The infantry was to search and destroy the Japanese positions on the high ground above the road, while tanks covered them as much as they could from the road. During their progress, First Lieutenant

F

1. TYPE 97 CHI-HA (EARLY), 26TH TANK REGIMENT

The fan symbol on this vehicle indicates the tank previously belonged to the 2nd Tank Regiment. It was one of the 22 replacement vehicles sent to Iwo Jima during the second half of 1944 to rebuild the 26th Tank Regiment's strength. the tank shows the pre-1942 jungle camouflage.

2. TYPE 97 SHINHOTO CHI-HA, 26TH TANK REGIMENT

This vehicle is showing the late camouflage pattern used on Japanese tanks, made of large splotches of dark and light brown over grass green paint. The yellow disruptive stripe is no longer in use. This tank was a former tank dozer and was captured intact by US forces.

1

2

ABOVE LEFT
The Type 1 47mm antitank gun was considered the first modern Japanese-designed antitank gun. It could easily penetrate the armor of American tanks (except the front plate) with its armor piercing shell. American tank crews were impressed by the Japanese fire discipline and qualified it as excellent. Very few rounds were wasted by Japanese gunners. In most cases, when a round was fired, it reached its target. (NARA via Ed Gilbert)

ABOVE RIGHT
A 47mm shell hit a weak spot on the front armor plate of this A Company 5th Tank Battalion Sherman. The ball-mounted machine gun was aimed and destroyed, killing the assistant driver instantly and wounding the tank commander. (MCHD)

OPPOSITE
The additional protection provided by the 2x12 oak planks and reinforced concrete between the wood and the hull sides of the tank was not sufficient to prevent 47mm antitank rounds from penetrating. It, however, added considerable weight to the tank and reduced maneuverability in soft terrain. (NARA)

English's tank, the "Crispy," was hit at point-blank range by several antitank guns. In such a confined environment (only several hundred yards apart), the lumber and concrete protections proved worthless. The M4A3's engine was set on fire and crew compartment penetrated, but the driver, Corporal Russell Whisenant, was able to back the tank into a shell hole. Whisenant recalled: "I looked down and saw my [left] arm hanging over the brake pedals. Hadn't felt any pain and didn't even know it was off. There is nothing to do in a case like that but try and escape, so I had to crawl out of the top of the tank, run around behind it and jump in a shell hole."

Mutual support from tanks was impossible in such terrain. However, the Japanese were able to exploit the ground to their advantage, concealing antitank guns on reverse slopes, in ravines, and in low ground, forcing the American tank crews to venture forward and face them individually without any protection from the following vehicles.

First Lieutenant Bellmon and the crew of the "Count" ran into the same misfortune as had the "Crispy." The M4A3 had reached the vicinity of airfield No. 2 when it was repeatedly hit and immobilized by several armor-piercing rounds from 47mm antitank guns. The tank's armor was penetrated and the engine compartment started to burn. Bellmon recounted:

> One of the projectiles went through the chest of the gunner [*sic*, the loader], […] and another tore the leg off the gunner […]. Not knowing who was still alive and who was injured, I gave the order to abandon the burning tank. When the driver, bow-gunner, and I got on the ground, […] we realized that two of our tank members were still inside. Quickly I climbed back on the tank, discovered that the assistant gunner [loader] was dead and pulled the badly injured gunner [Sergeant James Haddix[6]] out of the tank. I helped him down to the ground, and we survivors crouched as the tank burned and the anti-tank fire flew.

Though the tank was immobile and burning, the Japanese gunners continued to target the wreck. A corpsman reached the group with a stretcher,

---

6   Tank personnel was initially trained at each role in order to replace combat casualties and keep tanks running: tank commander, loader, gunner, driver, and assistant driver. They then occupied the function for which they showed the better skills. On Iwo Jima, casualties in vehicles and personnel lead to continual crew reorganization from D+1 through the end of the battle. Haddix for example started the battle as a tank commander and ended up as a gunner in the depleted crew of the *Count*.

and the four men carried Haddix back to their own lines. Bellmon continued: "By the time we reached our lines, we were all so exhausted we could not speak. I was covered with so much gore from the body of the dead crewman that the corpsman mistook me for one of the injured."

Massed tank attack on airfield No. 2

A Corps attack was organized on February 24 in an attempt to break the island's inner defenses. If the Americans succeeded in breaking through this line, the rest of the island's defenses would collapse – or so they thought.

The main effort was placed in the center, on airfield No. 2. The freshly landed 21st Marines (from the 3rd Marine Division) would conduct the assault, spearheaded by the largest tank formation yet assembled in the Pacific by the US Marine Corps.

Elements of the three tank battalions, totaling some 75 tanks, were placed under the command of Lieutenant Colonel William R. Collins, the 5th Tank Battalion's Commanding Officer. Two columns of tanks were formed, extending from airfield No. 1 to the vicinity of airfield No. 2, using the two runways connecting the airfields.

However, the Japanese had anticipated the use of the runways by American tanks, and both tank highways were heavily mined and covered by antitank guns. The armored assault thus bogged down almost immediately: in the first few hours, the lead vehicles of both columns were destroyed, preventing the following tanks from progressing and reaching the second airfield.

The 21st Marines finally started the assault without tank support, resulting in heavy casualties. Eventually, it was found that the only way to bring tank support onto the second airfield was by using a single narrow road in the center, cut by a tank dozer during the previous days.

The two tank columns managed to return to airfield No. 1 and formed a single file extending from one airfield to the other. At last, by early afternoon, the first tanks stumbled onto the second airfield and were able to provide efficient support to the battered 21st Marines. The initial attack had started at 0915hrs.

Of the 75 tanks that were mustered for the attack, about 17 were either damaged or completely destroyed. Despite their sacrifice, by the end of the day, the second airfield was still held, for the most part, by Japanese soldiers. The airfield was only considered secured by February 27.

The defense of airfield No. 2 was a Japanese tactical success, since they were

The "Crispy" belonged to 1st Lt Gearl M. English of 3rd Platoon, C Company, 4th Tank Battalion. The tank dueled a Type 1 antitank gun and was knocked out after being hit repeatedly, penetrated and set afire. Its driver was badly mutilated in the process despite the addition of wood, concrete, and steel on the tank sponsons. Note all the track blocks on the front slope were shot-up. (From the collection of Sergeant Major Bert Nave)

This withdrawing tank is taken under fire by an antitank gun on the northern taxi strip leading to airfield No. 2. The taxi strips were mined and covered by a multitude of guns, thus denying the access to tanks. (NMPW)

Well often tanks conducted rescue missions of wounded infantrymen on the battlefield. The tank would drive and position itself above the wounded Marine, drop its bottom escape hatch and the casualty would be lifted inside the crew compartment. Back to the friendly lines, the wounded was extricated from inside via the turret. Note the additional armor of this tank consisting of a plywood board on its side and steel tracks on the turret. (NARA)

able to delay the action of US tanks, making its capture very costly to American forces. Moreover, contrary to American expectations, the island of Iwo Jima did not fall after the capture of the second airfield. Indeed, there would be another four weeks of hard fighting before the island would finally be declared secured on March 26.

Unconventional tactics

Most terrain on Iwo Jima was considered unsuited to conventional tank action, especially in the north of the island. New combat techniques were thus designed for section- or platoon-size actions, since no larger tank formation could be employed at one time on the rough landscape. It was often necessary for tank dozers or armored bulldozers to cut new roads in the difficult terrain.

In such a confined environment, tanks were vulnerable to Japanese tank-hunter teams, particularly when the accompanying infantry had been pinned down by machine-gun or antiaircraft fire, forcing the tanks to advance without cover.

Sergeant Myron Czubko was the loader in the C Company, 5th Tank Battalion, tank dozer named "The Avenger." Czubko's tank was sent to clear a road into a ravine, while other tanks were in defilade to cover it. He recalled:

We were gone clearing out stuffs on that one particular time and it was between two ridges. Just before we went down in there, I looked through my periscope and I could see Japanese, kind of picking over the top to see where we were. We drive down in there and unfortunately we couldn't talk through our radio 'cause something went haywire on it. But we could hear. All of a sudden we hear a loud holler and yelling on that radio. Our tank driver [...] he heard all that noise and put that tank into reverse and out of there we came. I looked ahead and there was a gigantic splotch of lime colored stuff out there. They had thrown a charge under our tank and the guys behind us saw that so that's why they were yelling.

Even if tanks survived suicide attacks, they still faced other threats such as landmines and antitank guns. Disability rates were high, with only about 60 percent of the Shermans being kept functional at a time, the other 40 percent undergoing maintenance or having been destroyed.

It was common for individual tanks to be knocked out and repaired several times during the fighting on the island. Crewmen would rotate from one tank to another, as repaired vehicles were made available by the overbooked mechanics.

In A Company, 5th Tank Battalion, Private Martin Murphy fought in six different tanks, losing five to Japanese mines, shells, or satchel charges thrown under the tank. He recalled:

We only had two close calls: one [37mm] shell hit the side of the tank [and got stuck in the steel, the

This picture was taken on 25 February 1945, during the second day's attack on airfield No. 2. Here, tanks of A Company 3rd Tank Battalion are seen supporting Marines from F/2/9. Note the steel plate welded on the tank sponson as a unique additional protection against Japanese antitank weapons. In the background are tanks from the 4th Tank Battalion lost the day before. (NARA)

nose of it protruding inside the tank], one inch away from a five gallons can of gas held in the sponson. If that shell would have come through, it would have exploded and light[ed] up the gas, that would be the end of us.

Murphy did not attribute their survival to the lumber put on the sides of the tanks: "That wouldn't stop the shell, that would only stop the magnetic mines."

He added: "At the end [of the battle], in the sixth tank, we hit a 500pound aerial bomb. We had a bulldozer blade in front of it. We were dozing a road [...] and hit that bomb. The bulldozer blade was sent about ten feet away from the tank." Despite the terrific explosion, the tank was still running.

When the Japanese succeeded in disabling a tank, two options were available to the surviving American crews. They could either stay in the tank and turn the vehicle into a pillbox, and continue fighting, or else abandon the vehicle, depending on the situation.

Japanese soldiers were even known to occupy disabled vehicles. Consequently, when American crews were forced to leave their Sherman, they had to remove the firing mechanism from the tank weapons to render them inoperative. Myron Czubko explained what happened when his tank was disabled after running over a mine:

Just before we left that tank we were mandated to pull up all the firing pins out of the cannon and out of the machine guns. But someplace down the line, I guess somebody neglected to do it with their tank because the Japanese got those firing pins. They put it into our tank and turned the turret around and when the [maintenance] guys came in to retrieve our tank they started shooting at them with our gun. So they just backed off and they totally obliterated our tank after that.

Japanese tank actions

Contrary to what is commonly accepted in the West, the 26th Tank Regiment's defense of Iwo Jima was not entirely static, but rather active.[7]

7   The map on page p13, section "Technical factors" further attests the mobile nature of the Japanese tank defense on Iwo Jima, presenting the initial tank force location and the final destruction site of each individual Japanese tank on the island.

Due to terrain limitations, most of the time the tank platoon (three tanks) was the largest formation used to provide close infantry support on Iwo Jima. Here, a platoon of C Company 5th Tank Battalion works in close coordination with riflemen from the 3rd Battalion, 28th Marines. (MCHD)

The first attested Japanese armored reaction to the US landing occurred in the early hours of February 21.[8] It consisted of a local night counterattack conducted by a platoon of three tanks from the 2nd Company of the 26th Tank Regiment against the lines of the 3/23 Marines on the northern end of airfield No. 1.

The attackers were quickly dispersed when Marines accurately directed artillery on the advancing vehicles. One of them, a Type 97 Chi-Ha, was disabled and later captured by US forces, while the other two retreated without causing any damage.

The 1st and 2nd Companies took part in the defense of the second airfield, respectively in the eastern and western sectors. During this phase, Japanese tanks unquestionably fired at advancing Marine Shermans. Their performance, however, cannot be assessed due to a lack of records. The 1st Company conducted efforts to defend Hill 382, where it lost two tanks. One of them, a Type 97 Shinhoto Chi-Ha, fell victim to the 75mm cannon of an M4A3.

On February 27, B Company of the 4th Tank Battalion was supporting the attack of the 1/23 Marines against Hill 382. In his tank named "Bandit," Sergeant William H. Edgar got word that an enemy tank was holding up the infantry's progress. Edgar recounted: "We moved forward [...] but we had a hard time finding it. It was down in a revetment and was being used as an artillery piece to fire upon our troops." When the Type 97 was finally discovered by the tank crew, it was knocked out with a single 75mm round.

That same day, a section of Shermans from the 3rd Platoon of B Company, 5th Tank Battalion, attacked pillboxes in the vicinity of Hill 362A and destroyed an entrenched Type 97 Chi-Ha from the 2nd Company, 26th Tank Regiment.

"The Jap gun and the bulldozer tank fought a furious duel for a few minutes, and when the smoke and debris from the explosions cleared, the dozer had been immobilized and the Jap gun silenced." Unsuited terrain forced armored dozers and tank dozers to open roads to reach targets like here, in the vicinity of the village of Minami, in the 4th Division zone of action. (NARA)

8   Japanese sources indicate elements of the 1st Company were deployed in the area of the Quarry against 4th Division troops as early as the morning of February 20, but the involvement of tanks in this action is not attested.

When it became obvious that the second airfield could no longer be held, the 2nd Company redeployed to the sector of Motoyama village during the night. It then conducted a surprise daytime attack against riflemen of the 3/21 Marines on February 28. Bazooka fire and aerial support resulted in the destruction of five more Japanese tanks. The 2nd Company's commanding officer, Captain Isao Nishimura, was strongly criticized by Nishi for wasting his tanks in this daylight counterattack. The captain, accepting responsibility for his actions, committed suicide a few days later.

The next day, March 1, the 3rd Company (which had been held in reserve south of airfield No. 3) was holding the advance of the 1/21 Marines until US tanks from B Company, 3rd Tank Battalion, were called in support. The Japanese tanks were spotted at 1102hrs by Marine tankers. Thirteen minutes later, eight Japanese tanks were reported destroyed, seven of which had been hidden in revetments. The 3rd Company was thereby annihilated.

Surviving Japanese tanks regrouped in the vicinity of Nishi's CP, where they conducted the final defense in what would become known as Cushman's pocket. Little by little, they fell victim to constant shelling by naval guns, artillery, and rockets. Three more were eventually destroyed by 3rd Division's Shermans. Finally, the last surviving Japanese tanks were abandoned by their occupants for lack of ammunition, and were captured intact by American forces.

The most unusual Japanese tank action of the fighting on Iwo Jima occurred on March 10 in Cushman's pocket, involving a Japanese-manned Sherman. That day, a platoon of Shermans from B Company, 3rd Tank Battalion, was supporting the advance of the 3/21 Marines when Sergeant John O'Hara's tank was fired at by a Sherman from C Company, 3rd Tank Battalion. The C Company tank had been knocked out the previous day and occupied during the night by two Japanese soldiers, who familiarized themselves with the firing mechanism under cover of darkness.

ABOVE LEFT
The flamethrower tanks were considered the best suited weapons to reduce Japanese emplacements in the rugged terrain of Iwo Jima. Here, a flame tank from C Company, 4th Tank Battalion is used by the 5th Marine Division in mop-up operations in the north of the island. (NARA)

ABOVE RIGHT
Besides the flame tank, the dozer tank was considered one of the most valuable weapon in the US victory over Iwo Jima. Only nine were available on Iwo Jima. This is Myron Czubko's tankdozer, "The Avenger," acting in support of the 28th Marines somewhere on Iwo. (USMC HD)

G   5TH TANK BATTALION'S SHERMANS

The well-constructed Japanese fortifications resisted the 75mm cannon fire of the conventional Shermans. The use of flamethrower tanks was often the only way to definitely silence a strongpoint. A flame tank commander described how the specialized tank was used: "After the infantry designated some targets for the other tanks, they would fire a few rounds of 75mm in them. Then, we [the flame tank] in turn would move up and burn the target out." Tank crews reported that Japanese soldiers ran out of their emplacements when they spotted the first burst of flames from one of the specialized vehicles, only to then fall under a hail of machine-gun fire. The red triangles painted on the turret tops of these 5th Tank Battalion's Shermans were used by aerial reconnaissance to identify the front line.

RIGHT
View from atop the turret of a Type 97 Shinhoto Chi-Ha entrenched at the base of Hill 382 and overlooking airfield No. 2. From such a vantage point of view, it was easy for Japanese tankers to target approaching American tanks. (NARA)

FAR RIGHT
Several Japanese tanks such as this Type 95 Ha-Go were captured intact and brought back by American forces as war trophies. This vehicle shows the 26th Tank Regiment symbol painted on the turret. The original white colored insignia was painted over with dark paint to render it less visible. (NARA via Ed Gilbert)

During the course of the battle, Japanese tanks frequently changed emplacements to better attack US ground troops. Tank maneuvers occurred during the night to prevent detection from aerial observers. If spotted, American firepower had a devastating effect on Japanese armor. When moving, tanks also towed artillery pieces (the regiment's Type 90s) toward alternate positions of fire. (NARA)

A B Company tank crew stated: "The Japs fired a shell 75mm […] that was high explosive. It blew in contact [exploded outside], alongside the gunner side of the turret. Shrapnell [*sic*] from inside [the] turret killed Birtcil [Corporal Mervin P. Birtcil, gunner]. If this would have been an armor piercing 75mm shell, all five crew men would be dead." The four survivors managed to escape under a hail of machine-gun fire before a bazooka team finally silenced the Japanese-occupied C Company Sherman. Japanese sources claim that one of the two occupants of this Sherman was Second Lieutenant Ishiro Otani from the Artillery Company of the 26th Tank Regiment.

Survivors of the 26th Tank Regiment continued to put up a stubborn resistance against the Marines of the 3rd Division until Cushman's pocket was finally declared captured by American troops on March 16. Though their tanks were no longer operable, Nishi's men kept fighting for several more days with only light weapons and explosives, rushing at advancing American armor. The last survivors eventually escaped the pocket and worked their way to the north of the island, where they kept fighting even after the island was reported captured on March 26.

CONCLUSION

The battle for Iwo Jima is known for having been costly in human lives to both sides. The American losses were for the first time superior to those of the Japanese. Iwo Jima cost some 28,000 US casualties, while the Japanese garrison was annihilated, with some 21,000 military and civilian personnel killed and only a thousand captured alive.

Protected by the steel of their tanks, the men of the three Marine tank battalions suffered 17 percent casualties, far below the figure for other combatant units (about 60 percent).

The presence of the additional armor protection cannot be considered to have influenced the casualty rates for the tank personnel. The 3rd, 4th, and 5th Tank Battalions suffered 19 percent, 18 percent, and 14 percent casualties, respectively.

During previous Pacific battles, most casualties among tank personnel occurred while they were outside their vehicles. For example, only 35 percent of all the casualties sustained by

the 1st Tank Battalion on Peleliu occurred inside the tanks. This changed on Iwo Jima, where an estimated two-third to three-quarters of the casualties occurred inside the tanks.

U.S. tank personnel statistics					
Unit	Personnel strength	KIA/DOW*	WIA/sick/combat fatigue	MIA	Tank personnel casualty rate
3rd Tank Battalion	601	20	95	1	19%
4th Tank Battalion	687	24	98	0	18%
5th Tank Battalion	589	16	66	0	14%
Totals	**1,877**	**60**	**259**	**1**	**17%**

* Died of wounds

Neither does field-expedient armor seem to have been influential as regards the number of operable vehicles during the fighting. An average 60 percent of the US tanks in each battalion were kept operational at any time of the battle.

Furthermore, when the three tank battalions departed Iwo Jima they all had a comparable amount of tanks destroyed beyond repair: 30 percent for the 3rd Tank Battalion, 21 percent for the 4th Battalion, and 35 percent for the 5th Battalion.

Most tank casualties were the result of mines, guns, or antitank guns. In the end, the best protection for tanks turned out to be the accompanying infantry.

Data on tank losses sustained at Iwo Jima				
Unit	Initial tank strength	Destroyed tanks	Operational tanks	Tank losses rate
3rd Tank Battalion	46	15	31	33%
4th Tank Battalion	53	11	42	21%
5th Tank Battalion	51	18	33	35%
Totals	**150**	**44**	**106**	**30%**

Contrary to what was expected, the gasoline-powered M4A3 was no more prone to fires than the diesel M4A2. Until Iwo Jima, the twin diesel engine of the M4A2 was cherished for its reliability against the numerous infantry-borne ordinances fired at the engine bay of the tanks. When one engine was knocked out, the other could compensate and bring the tank back to friendly lines. Furthermore, when fuel cells were cracked, the diesel fuel tended not to burn immediately, leaving time for the crew to evacuate.

All these principles changed on Iwo Jima with the increased use of artillery and antitank guns by the Japanese defenders. Projectiles now penetrated crew compartments, where in addition to mutilating the crew, they often set the ammunition on fire. The huge advantage of the M4A3 issued to the Marines for Iwo Jima over the M4A2 was the presence of wet stowage bins to store

A Type 97 Shinhoto Chi-Ha left intact by its crew inside a revetment on Iwo Jima, possibly within Cushman's pocket. This is one of the 22 replacement tanks issued to the 26th Tank Regiment by late 1944. This particular vehicle is today preserved in the United States. (NMPW)

Iwo Jima was the first campaign during which Japanese made an extensive use of mines. They were the most common cause of US tank losses. Thought temporary, they significantly delayed American advance by cutting infantry from a valuable source of support. (From the collection of Sergeant Major Bert Nave)

main gun ammunition. These bins, in addition to being moved from their initial position in the sponsons to the tank floor, contained a fire retardant. When punctured, the retardant came in contact with the ammunition, thus delaying fires and giving a few precious seconds for the crewmen to evacuate the vehicle.

The Japanese 26th Tank Regiment was decimated on Iwo Jima. However, Lieutenant Colonel Nishi's strategy to conceal its small contingent of tanks in prepared positions was probably the best possible move, considering the superior American firepower, along with sea and air supremacy. Japanese tankers were well trained but suffered from political choices that neglected the development of armor during the previous decade.

Japanese tanks on Iwo Jima were not only obsolete, they also suffered from logistical issues due to the use of various models. As previously pointed out, several tanks were simply abandoned by their crew for lack of ammunition. With a reduced number of tank variants, the Japanese could have switched ammunition from disabled vehicles to those still running. Though it would not have changed the result of the battle, several tanks could have been kept operable a little longer if the number of tank variants had been limited. With four different types of main guns (see table "Iwo Jima armor technical characteristics", p. 11), this was simply impossible.

It is estimated that as of March 10 – the date on which the unit's records were destroyed – the 26th was a tank regiment in name only. Survivors thereafter fought a battle of attrition with only light weapons. Personnel from the 26th Tank Regiment eventually evacuated the trap of Cushman's pocket to continue fighting in the north of the island. In the end, only 20 men from the 26th Tank Regiment were taken prisoner. The rest of the personnel, including Nishi, died on Iwo Jima.

American victory on Iwo Jima relied on several industrial factors, with the mass-produced tank – and particularly the flamethrower tank – being judged "the best single weapon of the operation" by the Marine infantry.

Following Iwo Jima, the military strategies of both the Japanese and the Americans remained unchanged. The Japanese again employed in-depth defense on Okinawa to make the US victory there as costly as possible. Iwo Jima convinced the Japanese that the tank was the spearhead of American military force in the Pacific. Every attempt was thus made to slow American progress by attacking its armored formations.

As on Iwo Jima, the Japanese tank force on Okinawa was too small and obsolete to hope to turn the tide of the battle. Most advanced Japanese tank designs were kept for the defense of the homeland.

Meanwhile, the American combined arms doctrine in the Pacific remained the same. Several changes were, however, adopted in the organization of tank formations, with an increased number of spare tanks taken with the invasion force to replace destroyed vehicles in the field. The number of specialized tanks – such as recovery vehicles, tank dozers, and flame-tanks – was also significantly increased.

The M4 Sherman remained in service within the Marine Corps until it was gradually replaced by the long-awaited M26 in Korea in 1950.

Surviving tanks

After Iwo Jima was captured by the Americans, Marine Shermans used during the campaign were either scrapped or dumped into the ocean. Japanese tanks fared a similar fate. Of the tanks that were left on Iwo Jima, several had been booby-trapped with explosives by their crew and were dynamited by American engineers to prevent accidents. Those that were captured intact and brought back to the United States ended up scrapped or used as targets on firing ranges. Despite this, four tanks are known to have survived the post-war era and have an historical connection with the legendary battle.

One M4A3 is still on Iwo Jima. This vehicle was pushed into and buried in a hole after the battle was over. It was rediscovered and excavated when the Japanese conducted construction work in the early 21st century. Today, it is a key monument for those who travel to and visit the battlefield. This particular vehicle belonged to C Company, 4th Tank Battalion, and was named the "Count." It was commanded by First Lieutenant Henry Bellmon when it was destroyed by a 47mm antitank gun, south of airfield No. 2, on February 23, 1945.

Another M4A3 that belonged to A Company, 5th Tank Battalion, was brought back Stateside and used as a target on a shooting range. It was eventually purchased by a private collector, who sold it to a private company in Las Vegas, Nevada. The tank was then restored to running and firing condition. The identity of this vehicle remains unknown. It was one of the 24 Shermans of the 5th Tank Battalion that were modified to accept the bow-mounted E4-5 flamethrower: the additional steel plate welded on its right sponson is still in place.

The National Museum of the Marine Corps, Quantico, Virginia, possesses an M4A3 that used to belong to C Company, 5th Tank Battalion. The vehicle was brought back from Iwo to Hawaii and converted to a POA-CWS-H5 flamethrower tank in the summer 1945. Left rusting in a training area of Camp Lejeune (North Carolina) for decades, it was salvaged by the Marine Corps in the 2000s. The vehicle is awaiting restoration.

Lastly, a Type 97 Shinhoto Chi-Ha captured on Iwo Jima is today preserved at the US Army Ordnance training support facility at Fort Lee in Virginia. It was previously kept at the Aberdeen Proving Ground in Maryland. It was one of the 22 tanks shipped to Iwo Jima in late 1944 to reinforce the island's garrison. After the war, it was used to educate military personnel and had openings cut in the turret and sponson armor. Later, these holes were patched with steel plates. This particular vehicle had been converted by the Japanese to a tank dozer but was shipped to Iwo Jima without its blade.

This Type 97 Shinhoto Chi-Ha preserved at Fort Lee, Virginia is a veteran of the battle of Iwo Jima. The tank is portrayed on p. 33 with its original camouflage, and pictured on Iwo Jima on p. 43." (Eury J. Cantillo/Spencer Van Gils)

BIBLIOGRAPHY

Interviews

Czubko, Myron, interview by Romain Cansière (September 2, 2018)

Gilbert, Oscar E., interview with Joe Bruno, Katy, Texas (undated)

Murphy, Martin, interview by Romain Cansière (June 13, 2019)

Satkovich, Michael, John C. Carey Oral History Interview, Marine Corps History Division, Quantico, Virginia (November 30, 2006)

Letter

Murphy, Thomas F., *Letter to Mrs Patricia Mullen, archivist*, Marine Corps University Archives (July 2, 1998)

Articles

CINCPAC-CINCPOA, "Capabilities of the 47mm Antitank Gun" in *Weekly Intelligence*, Volume I, No. 51 (July 2 1945), p. 31

CINCPAC-CINCPOA, "Enemy Antitank Fire on U.S. Tanks", in *Weekly Intelligence*, Volume. I, No. 45 (May 14, 1945), pp.30–31

CINCPAC-CINCPOA, "Preliminary POW Interrogation Report No. 152" in *Translations and Interrogations Number 34* (June 27, 1945), pp. 139–148

CINCPAC-CINCPOA, "Preliminary POW Interrogation Report No. 183" in *Translations and Interrogations Number 39* (August 30, 1945), pp. 119–126

Books

Cansière, Romain & Gilbert, Oscar E., *USMC M4A2 Sherman vs Japanese Type 95 Ha-Go, The Central Pacific 1943–44*, Duel 108, Osprey Publishing, Oxford (2021)

Director of Intelligence, Army Service Forces, *Special Technical Intelligence Bulletin No. 9*, War Department, Washington D.C. (June 2, 1945)

Estes, Kenneth W., *Marines Under Armor: the Marine Corps and the Armored Fighting Vehicle, 1916–2000*, Naval Institute Press, Annapolis, MD (2000)

Garand, George W. & Strobridge, Truman R., *The History of the U.S. Marine Corps Operations in WWII, Volume IV: Western Pacific Operations*, Marine Corps Historical Division, Quantico, VA (1971)

Gilbert, Oscar E., *Marine Tank Battles in the Pacific*, Combined Publishing, Conshohocken, PA (2001)

Harper, David E., *Tank Warfare on Iwo Jima*, Squadron/Signal Publications, Ellijay, GA (2008)

Horie, Yoshitaka, *Explanation of Japanese Defense Plan and Battle of Iwo Jima*, ChiChi Jima (January 25, 1946)

King, Dan, *A Tomb Called Iwo Jima: Firsthand Accounts from Japanese Survivors*, Pacific Press, Nampa, ID (2020)

McCormack David, *Japanese Tanks and Armoured Warfare 1932–45: a Military and Political History*, Fonthill Media, Stroud, England (2021)

Military Intelligence Division, *Japanese Ammunition Part IV 25mm–70mm*, War Department, Washington D.C. (July 20, 1945)

Military Intelligence Division, *Japanese Tank and Antitank Warfare*, War Department, Washington D.C. (August 1, 1945)

Morishita Satoru, *History of the 26th Tank Regiment: Regimental Commander Nishi Fallen on Iwo Jima and the Desperate Battle of the Tank Unit*,

Imperial Army and Navy History Group, Electronic version (December 8, 2020)[9]

Ness, Leland, *Rikugun: Guide to Japanese Ground Forces 1937–1945, Volume 1: Tactical Organization of Imperial Japanese Army & Navy Ground Forces*, Helion & Company Ltd, Warwick, England (2015)

Ness, Leland, *Rikugun: Guide to Japanese Ground Forces 1937–1945, Volume 2: Weapons of the Imperial Japanese Army & Navy Ground Forces*, Helion & Company Ltd, Warwick, England (2015)

Zaloga, Steven J., *Japanese Tanks 1939–45*, New Vanguard 137, Osprey Publishing, Oxford (2007)

Zaloga, Steven J., *M4 Sherman vs Type 97 Chi-Ha, The Pacific 1945*, Duel 43, Osprey Publishing, Oxford (2012)

Memoirs

Bellmon, Henry & Bellmon, Pat, *The Life and Times of Henry Bellmon*, Council Oak Publishing Co., Tulsa, OK (1992)

Neiman, Robert M. and Estes, Kenneth W., *Tanks on the Beaches: a Marine Tanker in the Pacific War*, Texas A&M University Press, College Station, TX (2003)

Yaffe, Bertram A., *Fragments of War: a Marine's Personal Journey*, Naval Institute Press, Annapolis, MD (1999)

Unpublished Memoir

Nave, Kirby & Nave, Bert, *My Life as Told to My Son* (2004)

Reports

Chemical Corps, *Portable Flame Thrower Operations in World War II* (December 1, 1949)

CINCPAC-CINCPOA, *Defense Installations on Iwo Jima* (June 10, 1945)

CINCPAC-CINCPOA, *IWO JIMA* (January 10, 1945)

, *Iwo Jima, 5th Marine Division Reinforced Action Report, 19 February to 26 March 1945 (and Annexes)* (April 28, 1945)

CINCPAC-CINCPOA, "Know Your Enemy!" in *Japanese Antitank Warfare* (June 11, 1945)

Observer's Report, USAFPOA, *Armored Operation on Iwo Jima* (March 16, 1945)

4th Marine Division Operations Report – Iwo Jima, 19 February to 16 March, 1945 (and Annexes) (May 24, 1945)

Parker, John E., *Combat Report M4A2 and M4A3 Medium Tanks, Pacific Theater of Operations, U.S. Marine Divisions, as Observed by Fisher Representative John E. Parker* (undated)

3rd Marine Division Reinforced, Iwo Jima Action Report, 31 October 1944 – 16 March 1945 (and Annexes) (May 11, 1945)

Thomas, William M. & Knox, Bert A., *Trouble for Tanks: Fourth Marine Division Tank Operation on Iwo Jima* (1945)

Websites

http://www3.plala.or.jp/takihome/ (Japanese tank expert Akira Takizawa's website)

https://m.facebook.com/100064682410355/ (page "Hallowed Ground: The Terrain of Iwo Jima" is an original study of the battle by Christopher H. Marks based on topography, using maps and aerial photographs)

9   Japanese text

INDEX

Note: Page locators in **bold** refer to plate captions, pictures and illustrations.